The
Marijuana Chef
Cookbook

S. T. Oner

GREEN CANDY PRESS

Published by Green Candy Press
San Francisco, CA
ISBN: 1-931160-05-8

Copyright © 2001 S. T. Oner

Front and Back Cover Images © 2001 Larry Utley
Interior Photos and Illustrations © 2001 www.arttoday.com

typography: yolanda montijo

This book contains information about illegal substances, specifically the plant Cannabis Sativa and its derivative products. Green Candy Press would like to emphasize that Cannabis is a controlled substance in North America and throughout much of the world. As such, the use and cultivation of cannabis can carry heavy penalties that may threaten an individual's liberty and livelihood.

The aim of the Publisher is to educate and entertain. Whatever the Publisher's view on the validity of current legislation, we do not in any way condone the use of prohibited substances.

Printed in Canada by Transcontinental

The
Marijuana Chef
Cookbook

Dedication

Dedicated to NORML and everyone who has fought
against the war on drug users.

Table of Contents

Chapter 1

Marijuana Through the Ages

Cannabis is the genus, or botanical name, for the hemp plant—otherwise known as marijuana, pot, weed, charas, ganja, kif, bhang, sinsemilla, mary jane... Hardy and versatile, the marijuana plant grows in many different temperate zones all over the world.

Although marijuana was one of the first cultivated crops, little is known about how the plant actually made its appearance in human history. Pinpointing the exact location or time period in which marijuana was first grown is next to impossible. Instead, archeological digs and early writings provide clues suggesting that its use as a source for food, fiber, and medicine has been ongoing since ancient times. Recoveries at various sites indicate that, for at least the last 8,000 years, humans have used every part of the marijuana plant in some manner.

In many parts of the world where cannabis is cultivated, people are either unaware of, or not predisposed to exploiting, the euphoric effects of the plant. Often, they are only interested in the plant's fiber, which is taken from the stalk and used to make hemp—a sturdy fabric capable of being transformed into many things including paper, rope, and clothing. But these examples barely hint at the magnitude of ways in which marijuana can be used. In fact, the Business Alliance for Commerce in Hemp has recorded more than 50,000 non-smoking commercial uses for the plant. It is likely that the euphoric properties of cannabis were first exploited for medicinal, religious, or spiritual uses.

ANCIENT WORLD

China boasts the earliest written record of cannabis, which is featured in the world's first pharmacopoeia—an official list of medicinal drugs published by the Chinese government more than 4000 years ago. In fact, the Chinese have a long tradition of marijuana use and list its seeds among their 'ancient' grains, along with soybean. The world's oldest piece of paper made entirely from hemp was also found in China, and dates back to between 140 and 87 BC. In the second century AD, it is recorded that a Chinese surgeon, Hua T'o, successfully used an anesthetic made from cannabis seeds and wine during an abdominal surgery.

Indian and Middle Eastern cultures were the next to embrace marijuana use. There is evidence that, in India, the plant has been used recreationally since 1000 BC. In the Middle East, marijuana was often grown to make hashish—a resin prepared from the flowering tops of the female cannabis plant—and smoked or chewed as an intoxicant. Hashish production flourished in this region, due in part to the ban on alcohol by Mohammed, the spiritual father of Islam.

While the marijuana plant itself thrives in North Africa, its use has been surprisingly rare throughout the continent. However, in some cultures along the Zambesi River Valley (in what would be the present day Congo), warriors used the plant to prepare for battle. In Morocco, where it is called kif, marijuana has enjoyed a wide acceptance and is smoked by a substantial number of adult males to this day.

A BRAVE NEW WORLD

In the "New World," marijuana has a history as diverse as the cultures that have inhabited the Americas. There is some indication that the Spanish may have brought the plant with them when they colonized South America, and would likely have grown it to make sails and rope. Another possible explanation for its appearance is that Asian Indians may have brought the drug with them during their forced migration to countries like Cuba and (what was) the East Indies. In North America, marijuana was grown mainly for the fiber in the stalk, known as hemp. In the American South, long before the revolution, hemp was the most widely planted and cultivated crop next to cotton. There are no written records describing its use as an intoxicant, and it appears that Americans did not discover its potential for recreation until much later—in the 20th Century.

A HIGHER PURPOSE: MARIJUANA AND RELIGION

Nearly every major religion (with the notable exception of the Judeo-Christian) lauds marijuana's spiritual benefits, or has advocated its use for sacred purposes. Contained within the earliest Vedic texts— holy to the Hindus and written between 1500 and 2000 BC—cannabis is referred to as a 'sacred grass'. The Hindus claimed that Shiva, or the Great Spirit, actually lived within the plant and believed that, when the plant was consumed, Shiva passed straight into the body. For the Hindus, the preferred method of ingestion was to turn the leaves, flowers, and stems into a liquid called bhang. There is a Hindu proverb that states:

"He who uses no bhang shall lose his happiness in this life and the life to come. In the end he shall be cast into hell. The mere sight of bhang, cleanses as much sin as a thousand pilgrimages. He who scandalizes the user of bhang shall suffer the torment of hell so long as the sun endures."

The plant was so central to this region that followers of Buddha claim that on the path to enlightenment, all Buddha ate was the marijuana plant and its seeds. As witnessed in their Tantras, the Buddhists believed that marijuana was a "potent means of disengaging the mind from its mundane associations, leading it up to the divinity".

Some Suffi sects of Islam consider eating hashish to be a vital component to the mystical search. Other people—such as an ancient nomadic tribe known as the Scythians—burned the seeds and plant in small huts as part of their funeral ritual. As recorded by the Greek historian Herodotus, the plant was burned and the "smell of it [made] them drunk, just as wine does us." According to Herodotus, the Scythians eventually wound up on their feet singing and dancing, under the intoxicating effects of the drug. The plant was used for both recreational and ritualistic purposes in Africa, particularly in the Zambesi Valley and Nigeria, where people believed that weed would transport a person to ecstasy, and that its psychoactive powers could transform the body and mind. The Rastafarians are another group famous for using marijuana as an intrinsic part of their religious practices. Like the Suffis, they believe that people must ingest the substance in order to properly commune with their god.

RECREATIONAL USES

When the plant began to spread through the West, European reactions were remarkably similar to those uttered by the religious east. Sir William O'Shaughnessy noted in 1877 that the high was:

"...of the most cheerful kind, causing the person to sing and dance, to eat food with great relish, and to seek aphrodisiac enjoyments. In persons of a quarrelsome nature it occasions, as might be expected, an exasperation of their natural tendency."

Artists from Rimbaud and Baudelaire to Burroughs and Kerouac used the same language to describe the drug's effects. Baudelaire and Gautier, famous French writers, were both members of a hash-eating club. They later wrote poems and first-person accounts of their experiences while under the influence. Burroughs and Kerouac were both beat writers, living on the fringes of society, but writers in more traditional fields also heralded marijuana's effects. The lively portrayals of "being high" described by such a wide variety of people help to explain why marijuana easily crossed over into the realm of recreational use. It was fun, and it left little or no lasting effect on the user, with the exception of a 'sluggishness'—cured easily with a cup of coffee. Stories abound of artists, musicians, writers, and even scientists being inspired when under the influence of marijuana.

MARIJUANA TODAY: THE GREAT DEBATE

Today, we can only estimate the number of marijuana users around the world. In 1894, the Encyclopedia Britannica estimated that more than 300 million people consumed the drug regularly. Official figures certainly vary from region to region. In America, it is estimated that at least 24 million people have tried the drug, and about 4 million people are habitual users. In the 20s and 30s, only a relatively small amount of the population had come into contact with marijuana. Jazz musicians were commonly perceived as being 'high' all the time. Louis Armstrong, the father of Jazz, is often quoted as saying he smoked weed every single day. It was also around this time that government began to take steps to make marijuana illegal.

Even after using the drug became a punishable offense, demand for marijuana did not stop. The number of marijuana users exploded during the sixties, largely due to the accessibility of cheap weed from Mexico. College students and hippies who had 'dropped out' of society were openly smoking in the streets of New York, San Francisco, and Washington, DC. The plant became accepted by youth seeking to rebel against a conventional society. This was in marked contrast to other, non-Western parts of the world where smoking a 'doobie' wasn't considered a political statement.

Although the use of marijuana as medicine is a hotly debated issue today, it was considered a necessity for centuries. In modern times, the plant was used in remedies in Europe up until the 50s, when a series of committees determined that prescribing the plant would cause harm. Today, new scientific evidence is being used to challenge these findings. Groups are especially active on this front in both England and the Netherlands.

In the United States, marijuana was prescribed for everything from arthritis pain, to neuralgia, to uterine hemorrhages until the beginning of the 20th Century. The first governmental commission to study the plant in the United States was conducted by the Ohio State Medical Society and cataloged over 25 different treatments that it considered best handled by marijuana. It was with the introduction of aspirin that doctors began to drop the plant from their own modern pharmacopoeias. To this day, the U.S. government continues to grow and supply 300 marijuana cigarettes a month to 8 patients, one of whom claims that his pot saved his eyesight in his fight with glaucoma.

As the authorities in Europe and America continue the fight to outlaw marijuana, there is a growing desire among citizens of these nations to use marijuana as medicine. However, research is still inconclusive, as it both proves and disproves the merits of marijuana, depending on what is considered. What cannot be disputed, however, are the actual benefits experienced by patients while on marijuana therapy. Surprisingly enough, marijuana is most often prescribed for its ability to induce the 'munchies'. People on a variety of medicines often suffer from a lack of appetite, which in turn hinders their ability to heal. Consequently, many doctors and patients are turning to marijuana as an appetite stimulant.

Whether eaten or smoked, used for practical, recreational, spiritual, or medicinal purposes, marijuana remains one of nature's most versatile and useful plants.

Chapter 2

Using Marijuana

There are many reasons why people choose to cook with marijuana, ranging from concerns about the health risks of smoking, to the convenience of being able to carry the drug discreetly. Some medical marijuana users prefer eating the plant to smoking it, since many are not recreational drug users or cigarette smokers, and are therefore not accustomed to inhaling. The resultant high from eating marijuana can be a very good experience in and of itself, and many people treating themselves with marijuana prefer to cook with the plant. When it is eaten, marijuana's effects range from mild to intense. While there have not been any recorded overdoses of marijuana when smoked, the effects of marijuana can be very intense when eaten. If not consumed in moderation, marijuana can induce dizziness, vomiting, and extreme anxiety. Knowing the potential effects that the drug can have on your body will help you weigh the benefits and risks of adding marijuana to your diet.

THC: THE MAIN INGREDIENT

The most potent of all the chemicals contained in marijuana is Tetrahydrocannabinol, or delta 9 THC. THC comes in many forms called isomers. The THC isomers are subgroups of cannabinoids (monoterpene compounds) of which at least 50 have been isolated. The interaction of these cannabinoids causes a high that varies from strain to strain and gives each plant its distinct scent. For example, some highs tend to be more euphoric, while others cause drowsiness and relaxation. When marijuana is eaten, depending on the ingestion method, the psychoactive effects are dramatically different due to the various pathways through which the chemicals are absorbed into the body.

When marijuana is smoked or inhaled, the THC transfuses almost instantly through the thousands of capillaries on the surface of the lungs. Increasing the contact with the capillaries increases the amount of THC in the smoke that will, in turn, be assimilated into the bloodstream. As a rule, marijuana smoke should be held in the lungs for at least twent seconds—and up to fifty seconds—in order to absorb the maximum amount of THC.

Once it is in the blood stream, the THC travels to the brain where it binds to certain receptors—receptors that appear to be designated specifically for this task.

The presence of these receptors is often used to bolster the theory that an ancient genetic link exists between humans and marijuana. Another school of thought maintains that THC mimics the natural chemical anandamide, which also binds to these receptors. Anandamide is found in areas of the brain that regulate memory, coordination of movement, and emotions. Most prescribed drugs attempt to duplicate the body's own chemical process but are decidedly not natural, whereas THC seems to be an all-natural drug that helps the body continue to function normally.

The direct transmission of marijuana from the lungs to the brain when it is smoked helps account for the quick onset of the high. This high wears off once the THC molecules no longer bind to the receptors. Ultimately, the same process occurs when marijuana is eaten, but there are important differences—the effects are multiplied. When marijuana is eaten, it is metabolized into a THC metabolite in the liver. The term 'metabolized' simply describes the body's process of changing and using a substance to best suit its needs—it is the process of digesting food and absorbing vitamins. When THC is metabolized, it changes into a compound called 11-hydroxy-THC. This new compound is at least 15% more potent than delta 9 THC. Therefore, when 11-hydroxy-THC hits the brain, a more powerful high is induced. The initial

23

effects can take a long time to set in, depending on how much food is already in the stomach, as well as the strength of the marijuana being used in the recipe. The effects, though, can last for up to five hours, or even longer. Since the food containing the drug may not be broken down all at once, the 11-hydroxy-THC high may surge in phases. When marijuana is eaten, users often report feeling an initial rush, followed by coming down, and then peaking once again. The change in THC's composition may account for the fact that vivid hallucinations and other wild effects are experienced after eating marijuana, whereas these reactions are relatively rare after inhaling it. The possibility of experiencing an intense buzz is often a favorable argument sighted by devoted marijuana eaters. This probably accounts for the reason why so many groups use the plant for religious purposes—the experience can be surreal.

MARIJUANA MASTERY: KNOWING THE RISKS

Now that you know how the drug works in your body, you should learn about the short and long-term effects of marijuana use. One point cannot be stressed enough:

Do not dose people without their knowledge! Make sure that anyone who is about to consume food containing marijuana is well aware of exactly what is involved. There are obvious reasons for this; the psychoactive properties of marijuana can be over-whelming (even for experienced users) if they are unaware of the oncoming effects. Also, there are times when being high for 6 to 8 hours may not be convenient or welcome. Another thing to watch out for is inadvertently using too strong a dosage. Make sure that people know if the dish is particularly strong—they might want to have just a small amount.

It is a good idea when cooking cannabis to have some marijuana-free food lying around. Even though you may have just eaten, the munchies do still occur, especially a few hours into the high. At that point you probably will not be looking to become any high-er, so eating some regular food would be wise. Plus, eating straight food—and sometimes taking a nap—can help relieve any unwanted reactions to the inten-sity of the high.

Cannabis highs are slightly unusual, as different strains can mimic the effects of many other psy-choactive drugs. Some weed can seem speedy, while other weed is much more mellow. In addition, each person's reaction can vary according to his or her individual chemical make-up. Although there are distinctions between the sativa (energetic, light) and indica (soporific, tranquil) states, marijuana does not generally fit into any of the normal psychoactive groups of depressants, stimulants, and hallucinogens. Instead, users fluctuate between these states, feeling at times energized and at other times sleepy. What will happen at any given time depends on many factors such as: what else has been consumed, how much marijuana was eaten, one's emotional state before using, and so on. Also, the amount of exposure to the drug will change how the body functions under the influence. Long-term users tend not to suffer certain side effects that commonly afflict first-time or novice users, such as red eyes. Of course, the chance of experiencing side effects depends on the quality of the pot being consumed. Even though studies have been conducted to determine and identify what takes place within the body, the results are either contradictory or meaningless. Basically, a combination of positive and negative effects will occur. Feelings of euphoria are common, as are increased mental energy and awareness. People seem to be more in touch with their surroundings and may experience a distortion of the senses; people feel as though time is playing tricks on them; they also tend to feel a general sense of mirth—often resulting in fits of laughter.

These effects are not necessarily always positive. The increased awareness of one's social environment can cause paranoia and distortion of time may lead to a sense of being out of control. However, it should be noted that a good deal of the paranoia is probably due to the fact that one is committing an illegal act. It can be upsetting to zone out and forget where things are, or forget what you were saying. Inexperienced smokers will often notice an increase in their heart rate. This can be accompanied by anxiety and in some cases panic. Every drug, including alcohol and caffeine, has side effects. It is important to know what effects may occur and to decide whether or not you believe that the drug is worth taking. The answer to this question will differ for everyone, but it is something that should be considered before ingesting any type of drug.

THE TRUTH IS OUT THERE: MARIJUANA RESEARCH

Due to marijuana's status as a "Schedule I" narcotic, it has been next to impossible to study the drug in a scientific manner for much of the last century. This has lead to contradictory, misleading and often anecdotal information being spread as the gospel truth. In fact, attempts to research marijuana's long-term effects have produced mostly inconclusive data from sources that have staked out clear positions. However, it can be safely said that repeated long-term use of the drug will have lasting effects on a person's brain and respiratory system. No one fully understands how the brain reacts to cannabis; however, brain scans show that the brain of a user is different after a few years of marijuana use when compared to that of a non-user. Exactly what this information implies is unknown. There is no proof that marijuana causes the death of brain cells, however it is unlikely that it does so to the same degree as alcohol—because it would therefore be measurable—as is the case when alcohol is consumed. Even if brain cell loss could be proven, there is no further link establishing a fundamental change in a person's behavior or intelligence. The same can be said about the rumored links between marijuana and mental illness. Though some people definitely "wig out" while on the drug, this behavior subsides as soon as the marijuana has ceased binding to the receptors—when the person has "come down".

Although marijuana has been never been shown to be physically addictive, there is probably a level of social addiction that occurs. In these cases, users will seek out cannabis because they have habitually done so—not to simply satisfy a physical craving. Some studies have tried to demonstrate that users become more aggressive and irritable when deprived of the drug. This could very well be true—coffee drinkers tend to experience similar reactions when lacking caf-feine. However, the rush to ban caffeine has not even begun. Some studies claim that long-term users suffer from what has been labeled 'amotivational syndrome'. This probably has as much to do with the particular user as it does with THC levels.

It is often reported that consuming the plant can lead to either a reduced libido and/or impotency. There is no basis to this claim of impotency whatsoever. But, like coffee drinkers, male cannabis users have been shown to produce a relatively higher amount of two-tailed sperm. When viewed as a percentage of the total amount of sperm produced, however, they are statistically insignificant. The typical human male produces millions of sperm in one day, and barring any pre-existing conditions, will produce millions more the next day.

COMMON EFFECTS OF MARIJUANA

Red eyes	Muscle relaxation
Increase in appetite	Vertigo, dizziness,
Altered sense of time	vomiting
Dry mouth	A depressed feeling
Heightening of senses	Relaxed inhibitions
Laughter, general mirth	Sensation of anxiety,
Drowsiness	confusion, paranoia
Hallucinations	

An important thing to consider when hearing claims and reading studies about marijuana is that most

29

research has been performed on heavy users. Since the definition of the 'recreational user' varies for everyone, and since we each have a unique biochemistry, it would be foolhardy to accept any study (whether favorable or negative) as the final word. Much more research is needed, and in some countries—especially in Europe—that work is now underway.

TO EAT OR NOT TO EAT?

Concerns about the safety of smoking are very high, which is one reason why people prefer to cook with marijuana. The smoke from a joint contains three times more tar than a standard cigarette, and five times more carbon monoxide. This information, combined with the fact that marijuana smoke hits the lungs at a higher temperature, leads people to believe that cannabis smoke is more likely to cause respiratory disease or cancer of the lungs than tobacco smoke. However, marijuana does not contain nicotine—a drug that is thought to be even more addictive than heroin. While marijuana smoking is definitely not 'healthy', it should be noted that most pot smokers do not have the same 'pack-a-day' habits as cigarette smokers. One way to counteract the toxins contained in the smoke is to use a bong or waterpipe, which can help filter out some of the impurities and carcinogens. However, bongs are not very easy to conceal, and in many places the legal ramifications of having paraphernalia are equally as severe as having the plant in one's possession.

Of course nothing will minimize the effect of smoking as much as simply not smoking at all. Smoking pot may not be as convenient as eating it, especially for medicinal users, since the effects wear off sooner. It is not always possible to maintain your high if you smoke pot, especially if you are in a public place. There are many events that might be enhanced by a marijuana high, such as concerts, movies, and trips to the zoo, but these are not good places to light up. However, if you eat cannabis, there will be nothing to confiscate, and your high will continue.

MARIJUANA AS MEDICINE

People who use the marijuana plant for medical pur-poses (especially to relieve constant pain) often have to smoke up to five or six joints a day—a habit which may not be easily concealed from co-workers, the authorities, and others who might disapprove. Obviously if you are on the job, you don't want the entire staff to know about your marijuana use even if the drug has been prescribed by a doctor to alleviate your suffering. Many people still have not accepted the use of marijuana as medicine, and combating other people's personal bias when you are in pain is an unwelcome, additional stress. People who suffer from chronic pain may want to eat marijuana because the long lasting high enables muscle relaxation and relief. Recreational users typically want a high to kick in quickly. However, medical users might actually want a slower release of the drug into their system, since it enables the high to last longer. This may mitigate the extreme of the high, but consistent relief is what some consider most important. To achieve this, consider eating doses of marijuana with larger serving sizes. As the body breaks down the food, the marijuana will be released in stages—a process very similar to a 'time-release' capsule.

People have found marijuana to be effective in the treatment and relief of numerous ailments and terminal conditions. One of the first illnesses that pot was legally made available for was glaucoma. Marijuana has been proven effective in reducing ocular pressure, a condition that damages the eye over time. Glaucoma is the second leading cause of blindness in the United States, and most sufferers of the disease are not physically helped by the medications currently available. Unfortunately, most of these people do not live in areas where their doctors can prescribe marijuana. There are many glaucoma patients who credit their remaining eyesight to marijuana use. Other advocates include cancer patients undergoing chemotherapy, who use cannabis to stimulate their appetites. Their increased appetite helps them maintain the weight and strength to fight their illness. People living with multiple sclerosis, AIDS, and chronic migraines are all helped by marijuana's properties. Since most medicinal users don't want to smoke, for obvious health reasons, eating marijuana is their best option.

People may also choose to eat marijuana simply for economic reasons. Although you certainly can cook the flowers and the bud of the plant, it is just as effective to cook with the plant's leaves. The leaves are useless to the grower once the plant is harvested, and they have to be pruned off the plant. Be aware that leaves are still just as dangerous to have in your possession—the penalties for a pound of leaf are the same as those for a pound of bud—so the grower has an incentive to get rid of the leaves as soon as possible. But, because the leaves are harsh to smoke and are not nearly as high in THC, they are not very valuable and are often given away or destroyed as soon as possible. When cooked, the leaves will be stronger than their equivalent weight in buds.

Chapter 3

Marijuana Law

Throughout history, the marijuana plant has been praised and condemned like no other, and each attempt to ban its use has done little to curb its popularity. As early as 1378 AD, the Emir of India tried to discourage consumption of the plant by destroying crops and imprisoning users. He even went so far as to punish some offenders by pulling out their teeth. Over the next six hundred years, nearly every country in the world would enact laws to limit or ban the cultivation or use of cannabis. To this day, the international medical and legal communities continue to conduct forums on the humble hemp plant.

INTERNATIONAL OPINION

In the 1900s, many international commissions were convened to study the medical and societal effects of drugs and to develop guidelines for controlling and restricting their use. The International Opium Convention of 1912 was the most notable such commission, and nearly all European countries and the United States adopted its conclusions. In fact, only Great Britain and the Netherlands abstained from following the recommendations of the convention to "confine to medical and legitimate purposes the manufacture, sale and use of opium, heroin, morphine and cocaine".

In 1946, the United Nations Commission on Narcotic Drugs held its first session in which it was determined that marijuana did not pose a threat to users or to society in general. This landmark decision heralded a potential reprieve in the prohibition laws being enforced the world over. The report from the session cited the testimony of physicians in Mexico, the United States, and India who held the position that the cannabis plant was not harmful to the health of the user and that the use of cannabis did not lead to criminal activity. The Indian physicians contended that any harmful effects due to cannabis use were likely dependent upon the predisposition of the user.

Less than a decade later, a 1954 report by the World Health Organization (W.H.O.) declared that cannabis was medically obsolete and that use of cannabis was likely to lead to addiction. Internal commissions in many countries arrived at the same conclusion—most relying on anecdotal accounts that insanity and addiction were prevalent among users in the Middle

East and India. The only European country to ignore these findings was the Netherlands, which determined that cannabis consumption was no worse than that of alcohol and should be controlled in a similar manner.

For the next 10 to 15 years, there were two schools of thought on the legal issues surrounding marijuana. One group, lead by the Netherlands and including India and Egypt among others, contended that marijuana should be controlled, but not criminalized. They agreed that marijuana abuse was an addiction, but found this to occur only in small numbers of the population, at lower levels than alcohol addiction. The other school of thought, supported by much of Europe and the United States, contended that marijuana posed serious health and social risks and wanted to ban the drug immediately and to enforce harsh penalties on users and traffickers.

U.S. LAW: THE WAR AGAINST MARIJUANA USERS

In the United States, California was the first state to establish an anti-marijuana law in 1907[1]. U.S. Federal law did not take on marijuana use until much later,

---

[1] In 1907 marijuana was labeled a poison in California. In 1915 its possession was prohibited unless prescribed by a physician. It was not until 1929 that marijuana was included among 'hard narcotics' like morphine and cocaine. It is therefore interesting that California, among the first states to begin restricting the use of marijuana, would, nearly one-hundred years later, be leading the charge to legalize it for medicinal purposes.

with the introduction of the Marihuana Tax Act in 1937. The U.S. government's policy would only get more restrictive in the sixties and seventies when President Nixon's administration launched its all out 'War on Drugs.'

During the sixties the United States was in revolt. People were smoking marijuana at student protests where they were 'dropping out' of mainstream society. This, in combination with student protests in places like Kent State and the University of California at Berkeley[2], created an unfortunate connection. Marijuana smoking came to symbolize the rebellious, long-haired, free-love attitude that the authorities wished to stop. In addition, there was the suspicion that marijuana use lead to the abuse of harder drugs, such as heroin and cocaine. Nixon was especially disturbed by this behavior and made the elimination of marijuana from the streets a top priority.

The War on Drugs has been enormous both in cost and scope, and has done little to decrease actual drug consumption. Drug use in general—and marijuana use in particular—have increased since the sixties. One thing that the War on Drugs has achieved is the imprisonment of a large number of non-violent

[2] It is an interesting side note that the governor of California during this turbulent time was none other than Ronald Reagan. His reaction to the protest was swift and severe. He ordered the National Guard to take back the campus.

offenders. This has had a chilling effect on marijuana users. For instance, in 1998, over 700,000 marijuana-related arrests were made—88% of them for possession. According to NORML, the National Organization for the Reform of Marijuana Laws, an arrest is made for a marijuana-related offense every nine seconds. According to the FBI, one marijuana smoker is arrested every 52 seconds in America.

Harsher still is the "three strikes" law, which requires that long sentences be imposed on repeat offenders. This law was intended to keep violent criminals off the street, but non-violent marijuana users are a casualty. Due to the minimum sentencing guidelines of the law, there are quite a few people serving sentences of 10 to 15 years—or longer—for possession. Under the current system, judges are not given the discretion to limit sentences because the law includes sentencing provisions that they are forced to uphold.

What all of this makes clear, is that the U.S. government is actively fighting a war—not on drugs—but against its own citizens.

THE TRUTH IS OUT THERE: DEBUNKING THE "GATEWAY" THEORY

Since before the 1950s, marijuana has been associated with the idea of "gateway" drugs. In 1955, one of the many advisory committees that convened in Europe to study cannabis first officially made this causal connection. A doctor from the W.H.O. stated that marijuana use leads to intravenous drug use and, ultimately, to serious drug addiction. Over the years, countless attempts have been made to prove that marijuana is the missing link in the progression to hard drug use.

The DEA web site lists the following 'statistical associations': "Twelve to 17 year-olds who smoke marijuana are 85 times more likely to use cocaine than those who do not. Sixty percent of adolescents who use marijuana before age 15 will later use cocaine."[3] One immediately wonders how many of these marijuana users did not use cocaine later on. Another troubling issue about these statistics is that it is unclear what exactly is meant by the term 'use'.

The truth of the matter is that there is a lot of information missing behind these statistics. In fact, when you take a broad view, the number of drug users has remained relatively constant over the last twenty years. What has increased, after a short dip, is the number of people who have experimented with drugs. Experimentation is not the same thing as habitual use. This would seem to indicate that the country's

---

[3] To quote Mark Twain: "There are three types of lies: white lies, damned lies, and statistics."

 40

youth are not on their way to becoming junkies.

Another thing that undermines the legitimacy of the gateway drug theory is the fact that nearly every-thing—from cigarettes and coffee to chocolate and sugar—could be a gateway drug. Lately, he media has devoted a lot of attention to the theory that cigarettes are in fact the gateway to marijuana, which in turn, is the gateway to a lifetime of drug abuse. If only causal associations are necessary, then everything from sugar to caffeine is surely a candidate for gateway drug-dom. This, as it turns out, is not said entirely in jest. Three Italian researchers have "proven" chocolate to be a gateway drug. Apparently the chemicals in chocolate activate the same receptors that marijuana does. Like THC, these chemicals produce anandamide. It is precisely this effect that produces the insatiable craving for chocolate in some people. These chemi-cals have the ability to mimic cannabis's effects, but it would take at least several pounds of chocolate for one to feel stoned. Phenylethylamine is another stim-ulant found in chocolate, and it is related to the stronger stimulant class of amphetamines. These stimulants in general, and Phenylethylamine in partic-ular, affect the body's ability to be attentive and alert. Although there is almost no scientific basis to the gateway drug theory, we shouldn't expect it to be abandoned any time soon.

AVOID THE RAP: KNOW THE LAW

Whatever your reasons for using marijuana, the best way to protect yourself and your loved ones from potential arrest and prosecution is to find out as much as possible about federal and local law. A good place to start is on the Internet—since governments publish much of this information online. The penalties for possession and cultivation can change drastically depending on how much marijuana is involved, and can include possession of paraphernalia as well.

In some states, like California, amounts under one ounce are considered misdemeanors, whereas Utah and Nevada have zero tolerance laws (one seed is equivalent to a pound for all intents and purposes). There can be local differences even within states. In California, for instance, the laws are more lenient in Humboldt County than they are in Orange County[4].

Common sense is usually your best weapon, and can go a long way to keeping you out of harm's way. Avoid transporting marijuana whenever possible, and pay special attention to pipes and other devices. In every state in the union, the police can make an arrest for either the paraphernalia or possession, due to the resin that collects in the bowls. If you must carry pot, it would be wise to do so in a cooked

[4] For a complete list of schedules and their definitions, please see Appendix B.

form, or as a joint at the very least. Police dogs however, will not be fooled by a marijuana brownie.

DRUG TESTING IN THE WORKPLACE

Another threat that has emerged for marijuana users is the prevalence of drug testing in the workplace. Labeled by supporters as a means to increase attendance and productivity, and to identify which workers may need help, its use has exploded in recent years. Yet, the reality is that drug testing penalizes users with positive tests that can bear little to no relation to work performance—not to mention the likelihood of false positives. It also is a terrible invasion of privacy—as what is done away from the workplace should be of no business to the employer. Currently, it is estimated that as many as 80% of large companies, affecting 40% of U.S. workers, have implemented drug-testing programs.

What makes drug testing such a potent issue for marijuana users is the length of time that marijuana is detectable in the body. For infrequent users, the drug stays in the system and is detectable in urine for about two to five days. This number jumps to fourteen days for more regular users, those who use a couple of times a month. For regular users of marijuana, the drug can be traced through urine for up to two or even three months[5]. Because there are also many variables unique to the individual, it is nearly impossible to say with any certainty how long marijuana will stay in a person's system.

There are many types of tests that are currently in use, but most of them are horribly inaccurate—producing up to 30% false positives. They can be divided into four categories: urine tests, hair tests, perspiration tests, and residue tests. Of these tests, the most common is the urine test, because it is the cheapest to administer and to screen.

A FINAL WORD

The sharp increase in testing—both in the United States and across the world—seems to indicate that things are particularly bleak for marijuana users, but there are signs of change for the positive. Between 1978 and 1998, 34 states and the District of Columbia have passed laws recognizing marijuana's therapeutic values. Unfortunately, these laws do not trump Federal law. They do signal a significant shift in public opinion concerning marijuana. This trend is also sweeping Europe and beyond, where many countries are reviewing or revising their marijuana laws.

---

[5] There is a fairly common phenomenon that can occur with chronic users. Due to the body's familiarity with the drug it can pass through the user's system extremely quickly. There are many cases where negative results have been seen in unexpected surprise tests, despite the user having smoked all week.

Portugal has already decriminalized marijuana use, and New Zealand and Jamaica are not far behind. This is good news, especially to medicinal users, because the relaxation of prohibition could bring opportunities for renewed scientific study. Currently research is permitted in the United States—but only on a very limited basis—and by agencies that have clear motives.

Clinical trials and strong scientific evidence are needed in order for real change to occur in U.S. and international marijuana policy and law. There is no question that the burden of proof will be placed on those who support legalization and medical marijuana. All of this seems ironic when you consider the fact that the U.S. government currently grows and distributes marijuana to eight people for medicinal reasons. One of the eight is a long-term sufferer of glaucoma who credits his remaining sight to his regular use of marijuana.

Chapter 4

Cooking Basics

Unlike most other drugs, Marijuana is oil-based. Knowing this distinction is necessary when cooking with the drug. To ensure that marijuana's psychoactive properties are evenly distributed through the food. The THC of a marijuana plant is contained in the capitate glands that cover its leaves, but the flowers contain the highest density of the drug. Using an oil-product, such as butter or vegetable oil, does a fine job of dissolving the capitate glands and releasing the THC. So, it follows that making pot tea solely with water will not be as effective unless milk or honey is also used.

There are two basic ways to break down the plant for cooking—one is to make flour out of the leaves, and the other is to make marijuana leaf butter. To make the flour, you should grind very dry leaves in a food processor or coffee grinder until they are very fine. To make marijuana butter, simply combine about a pound of butter for every four ounces of marijuana leaf. Be sure to melt it down completely, and then strain the liquid from the mixture and store it in the refrigerator.

It is most common for people to add marijuana to desserts because desserts have a high fat content, are usually small serving sizes, and are very tasty in their own right. The fat is the key—it dissolves the plant's capitate glands and helps maintain even distribution throughout the food. When the serving size is smaller, the high will take effect much faster since there is less food to digest. One cookie, brownie, or even krispy treat, could contain all the drug desired.

When cooking with marijuana, make sure the dosage is correct—ingesting too much of the drug can leave you incapacitated. Since your aim is for people to have a good time, as a good cook you should pay special attention to dosage guidelines. Additionally, you want to make sure that the dose is spread out evenly in the food.

CALCULATING DOSAGE

Dosage has as much to do with the quality of the plant as it does with the individual body weights of the people who are eating the food, and their experiences with marijuana. Generally speaking, the concentration of THC in a plant is between 4 and 8 percent, though some high-grade products could be as high as 10 percent. Inexperienced users should stay within the lower ranges, eating less than 1/2 gram per serving. More experienced users can eat stronger servings, but should still be careful as they approach 1-1/2 grams.

As a general rule, eating 1 gram of pot will bring you to a peak in about two hours. Your peak will likely last for a couple of hours and then you'll start to come down. All in all, the effects of the marijuana will be felt for a total of 7 hours.

Be especially careful with dosage when substituting marijuana butter in a straight recipe, (one that does not call for marijuana). In these cases, the tendency might be to add a little more than necessary, which you should avoid doing. Remember—you can always eat more.

RECOMMENDED SINGLE DOSE FOR AN EXPERIENCED PERSON WHO WEIGHS 150 POUNDS*	
Marijuana butter	1/2 to 2 grams**
Marijuana leaf flour	1/2 to 2 grams

*For inexperienced users, the lower numbers should be sufficient.
**One half cup marijuana butter (1/4 pound) equals approximately 1 oz of marijuana leaf flour.

MARIJUANA BUTTER

Marijuana butter can be used in any number of recipes, from desserts to entrees and appetizers. For best results, marijuana butter should be prepared one full day before using.

RECOMMENDED DOSAGE	Approximately 4 oz. of leaf for every 1 lb. of butter
PREPARATION TIME	5 minutes
COOKING TIME	2 1/2 to 3 1/2 hours

1. Combine the butter and marijuana leaf in a large stockpot.
2. Add enough water to cover the leaf by a couple of inches.
3. Bring to a boil, stirring occasionally, to melt the butter.
4. Lower heat and simmer uncovered for 2 to 3 hours or longer to attain maximum extraction.
5. Allow mixture to cool slightly.
6. Pour through a fine mesh strainer and press the remaining liquid from the marijuana.
7. Transfer liquid to a container, cover, and refrigerate overnight.

MARIJUANA FLOUR

The easiest way to prepare marijuana for baking is to process either leaf or bud into flour. The only difference between leaf and bud is that the strength is different so the dosage will differ. Marijuana flour can then be added directly to recipes.

RECOMMENDED DOSAGE	1/2 to 2 grams per serving
PREPARATION TIME	10 minutes

1. Make sure that the marijuana is dry and crisp. Leaf and bud for flour should be dry enough to crumble easily between your fingers. For 20 grams of fresh leaf or 10 grams of fresh bud, roughly 10 minutes in a warm (200°F/90°C) oven or a minute or two in a microwave will suffice.
2. Remove any woody debris, stalks, stems, or seeds.
3. Place the marijuana in a food processor, blend it to a powder-like consistency, and let it settle. A coffee grinder works just as well when preparing small quantities of marijuana flour.
4. Using a knife, or other utensil, work the marijuana flour through a sieve to break down stubborn leaves and remove any remaining debris. You might notice a fine dust being thrown up during the process. This is precious, potent stuff, rich in THC. Hang onto it!
5. Marijuana flour should be stored in an airtight container and refrigerated.

MARIJUANA ALCOHOL

Another way to prepare marijuana is to use alcohol. Marijuana alcohol is the easiest way to process leaf and can be used to create an intoxicating and mouth-watering array of beverages. For more information, consult "Chapter 10: Drinks."

Chapter 5

Dessert First

If you're like me, dessert is the food you reach for first when you're enjoying marijuana in any form. It seemed perfectly natural, then, to blend marijuana and the following dessert classics to create the perfect treat to satisfy both your marijuana craving and the munchies. Take it from me, The Marijuana Chef, when you're cooking with cannabis always enjoy your Dessert First!

Gone Bananas Bread

SERVINGS	Makes one 9-inch loaf that serves 10
RECOMMENDED DOSAGE	10 grams of marijuana flour or 2 1/2 teaspoons of marijuana butter
PREPARATION TIME	5 minutes
COOKING TIME	Approximately 1 hour
INGREDIENTS	1 1/2 cups of all purpose flour 1 teaspoon of baking powder 1 teaspoon of baking soda 1/4 teaspoon of salt 3/4 cup of semisweet chocolate chips 3/4 cup of walnuts, toasted, chopped (optional) 1/2 cup (1 stick) of unsalted butter, room temperature 1 cup of sugar 2 large eggs 1 cup of mashed ripe bananas 1 1/2 teaspoons of vanilla extract 2 tablespoons of fresh lemon juice

DIRECTIONS

1. Preheat oven to 350°F/175°C.
2. Butter and flour a 9 x 5 x 2-1/2-inch metal loaf pan.
3. In a medium bowl, whisk the flour, baking soda,

baking powder and salt to blend.

4. Combine the chocolate chips (and walnuts) in a small bowl; add 1 tablespoon of flour mixture and toss to coat.
5. Beat butter in a large bowl until fluffy.
6. Gradually add the sugar, beating until well blended.
7. Beat in eggs one at a time.
8. Beat in mashed bananas, lemon juice and vanilla extract.
9. Beat in flour mixture.
10. Spoon 1/3 of the batter into the prepared loaf pan and sprinkle with half of the nut mixture.
11. Spoon 1/3 of the batter over top and sprinkle with the remaining nut mixture.
12. Cover with the remaining batter. Run a knife through the batter in a zigzag pattern.
13. Bake until the tester (a knife or fork inserted into the center) comes out clean—about 1 hour and 5 minutes. Turn onto a rack and allow to cool.

You'll go Ape for this Tasty Treat

Trippy Krispy Treats

SERVINGS	Makes approximately 24 squares or 12 servings
RECOMMENDED DOSAGE	3 teaspoons of marijuana butter
PREPARATION TIME	15 minutes
COOKING TIME	20 minutes on the stove or 3 minutes in the microwave
INGREDIENTS	6 cups of Rice Krispies cereal or other rice cereal 3 tablespoons butter 1 package of regular marshmallows (10 oz, about 40 marshmallows) or 4 cups of miniature marshmallows vegetable cooking spray chocolate chips (optional)

STOVETOP DIRECTIONS:

1. Melt butter in a large saucepan over low heat.
2. Add marshmallows and stir until completely melted. Add chocolate chips.
3. Remove from heat.
4. Add cereal and stir well until coated.
5. Using waxed paper or a buttered spatula, press the mixture evenly into a 13 x 9 x 2 inch pan coated with cooking spray. Leave out or put into fridge.

58

6. Cut into 2-inch squares when cool.

MICROWAVE DIRECTIONS:

1. Microwave butter and marshmallows on HIGH for 2 minutes in a microwave-safe bowl. Stir.
2. Microwave on HIGH for 1 more minute. Stir until smooth.
3. Add chocolate chips.
4. Add cereal and stir until well coated.
5. Press into pan and cool as directed in step 3 above.

Nuke Your Brain to a Krisp

Sweet Sensations
Sugar Cookies

SERVINGS	50 to 60 cookies, 30 servings
RECOMMENDED DOSAGE	15 teaspoons of marijuana flour or 6 1/2 teaspoons of marijuana butter
PREPARATION TIME	15 minutes
COOKING TIME	Chill 3 hours or overnight, then cook for 8 to 10 minutes
INGREDIENTS	3 lbs of all purpose flour 2 lbs of unsalted butter (room temperature) 1 lb of sugar, plus 1 cup for garnish 2 large eggs 1/2 teaspoon of vanilla extract pinch of salt

DIRECTIONS:

1. Preheat oven to 350°F/175°C.
2. Cream butter in a mixer until light and fluffy. Add sugar and continue mixing on high until the butter is soft and pale.
3. In a separate bowl, whisk together the eggs and vanilla. On low speed, add the eggs and continue to blend, occasionally scraping down the sides of the bowl to ensure proper mixing.
4. Add the flour and salt and blend on low speed until

the dough comes together and there is no trace of flour.

5. Cover in plastic wrap and chill until firm—3 hours or overnight.
6. Remove dough from refrigerator and allow to soften slightly—it will make it easier to work with.
7. Pinch off teaspoonful-sized pieces and roll into a ball. Drop into the sugar you reserved for garnish and coat.
8. Place on a cookie sheet lined with parchment paper and flatten slightly into a disk (with thumb).
9. Bake for 8 to 10 minutes or until lightly browned.

Surrender to the Sugar High

Outrageous Oatmeal Chip Cookies

SERVINGS	Makes approximately 48 cookies, 24 servings
RECOMMENDED DOSAGE	12 teaspoons of marijuana flour or 5 teaspoons of marijuana butter
PREPARATION TIME	15 minutes
COOKING TIME	10 to 12 minutes
INGREDIENTS	1 1/4 cups of brown sugar, firmly packed 1 cup of butter, softened 1/2 cup of sugar 2 eggs 2 tablespoons of 2% milk 2 teaspoons of vanilla 1 3/4 cups of flour 1 teaspoon of baking soda 1 teaspoon of salt 2 1/2 cups of quick-cooking oatmeal 12 oz of semi-sweet chocolate chips

DIRECTIONS:

1. Preheat oven to 350°F/175°C.
2. In a large bowl, beat brown sugar, butter and sugar until creamy.
3. Add the eggs, milk and vanilla. Beat well.

4. Stir in flour, baking soda and salt.
5. Mix in oatmeal and chocolate chips.
6. Drop by teaspoonfuls onto an ungreased baking sheet and bake for 10 to 12 minutes or until cookies start to brown.
7. Cool slightly before removing from baking sheet.

So Good They Oat to be Against the Law

Nutty Peanut Butter Cookies

SERVINGS	Makes 60 small cookies, 30 servings
RECOMMENDED DOSAGE	15 teaspoons of marijuana flour or 6 1/2 teaspoons of marijuana butter
PREPARATION TIME	15 minutes
COOKING TIME	10 to 15 minutes
INGREDIENTS	1/2 cup of butter 1/2 cup of brown sugar 1/2 cup of white sugar 1 cup of peanut butter 1 1/2 cup of flour 1 egg 1 teaspoon of salt 1/2 teaspoon of baking soda 1/2 teaspoon of vanilla

DIRECTIONS:

1. Preheat oven to 375°F/190°C.
2. Cream together butter, white and brown sugars.
3. Add the egg, peanut butter, salt and baking soda.
4. Mix flour into batter and add vanilla.
5. Roll dough into small balls and flatten with a fork dipped in water.
6. Bake for 10 to 15 minutes.

Nothing Could Be Better

Crazed Carrot Cake
(It's all in the frosting!)

Servings	Serves 20
Recommended Dosage	5 teaspoons of marijuana butter
Preparation Time	30 minutes
Cooking Time	35 to 45 minutes or until the center is done
Ingredients	2 cups of flour 2 cups of sugar 2 teaspoons of baking soda 2 teaspoons of cinnamon 1 teaspoon of salt 3 cups of grated carrots 4 eggs 1 teaspoon of vanilla extract 1 1/2 cups of vegetable oil Frosting: 8 oz cream cheese 1 stick of butter 1 tablespoon of vanilla extract 1 lb of powdered sugar

CAKE DIRECTIONS:
1. Preheat oven to 325°F/160°C.
2. Sift dry ingredients into a mixing bowl.
3. Mix in grated carrots, vanilla and eggs.

4. Beat mixture and slowly add oil.
5. Pour the batter into a buttered 8 x 12-inch pan, or two 8-inch diameter pans.
6. Bake for 35 to 45 minutes or until the center is done.

FROSTING DIRECTIONS:

1. Beat cream cheese, adding butter and vanilla.
2. While beating, add the powdered sugar in thirds.
3. Frost the cake and enjoy!

420 Vision

"Choc-ful-'o-Pot" Chocolate Chip Cookies

SERVINGS	Makes approximately 48 cookies, 24 servings
RECOMMENDED DOSAGE	12 teaspoons of marijuana flour or 5 teaspoons of marijuana butter
PREPARATION TIME	20 minutes
COOKING TIME	10 minutes or until edges are lightly browned
INGREDIENTS	1 cup of butter, softened 1 cup of packed brown sugar 1 cup of white sugar 2 eggs 2 teaspoons of vanilla extract 3 cups of all-purpose flour 1/2 teaspoon of salt 1 teaspoon of baking soda 2 teaspoons of hot water 2 cups of semisweet chocolate chips 1 cup of chopped walnuts (optional)

DIRECTIONS:

1. Preheat oven to 350°F/175°C.
2. Cream butter, white sugar and brown sugar together until smooth.
3. Beat in eggs one at a time.
4. Stir in vanilla.

5. Dissolve baking soda in hot water and add it to the batter along with the salt.
6. Stir in flour, chocolate chips and nuts (if desired).
7. Drop by large spoonfuls onto ungreased baking dish
8. Bake for about 10 minutes or until edges are lightly browned.

Melts in Your Mind, Not in Your Hands

Baked Brownies

SERVINGS	Serves 12
RECOMMENDED DOSAGE	6 teaspoons of marijuana flour or 3 teaspoons of marijuana butter
PREPARATION TIME	15 minutes
COOKING TIME	20 to 22 minutes
INGREDIENTS	3/4 cup of melted butter 1 1/2 teaspoons of vanilla 1 1/2 cups of sugar 3 eggs 1/2 cup of Hershey's cocoa (or comparable brand) 3/4 cup of flour 1/2 teaspoon of baking powder 1 cup of chopped nuts (optional) 1 cup of chocolate chips

DIRECTIONS:

1. Heat oven to 350°F/175°C.
2. Grease a 13 x 9-inch pan.
3. Beat eggs, butter, sugar and vanilla in a large bowl.
4. Mix in cocoa, flour, salt and baking powder and blend.
5. Stir in nuts and chocolate chips.
6. Pour into pan and bake for 20 to 22 minutes.
7. Cool, cut, and eat 'em up!

Unlike Mom Used to Make

Chapter 6

Soups and Starters

"Off Your Noodle" Soup

SERVINGS	Makes 6, 1 1/4 cup servings
RECOMMENDED DOSAGE	1 1/2 teaspoons of marijuana butter
PREPARATION TIME	20 minutes
COOKING TIME	20 to 25 minutes
INGREDIENTS	6 tablespoons (3/4 stick) butter 1 cup diced carrots 1 cup diced celery 1/2 cup chopped onion 1/2 tsp freshly ground pepper 1 1/4 cups sliced white mushrooms 6 cups chicken broth 1 cup cooked chicken cubes 2 cups cooked wide egg noodles 2 to 3 tbsps chopped fresh dill or parsley

DIRECTIONS:

1. In a large pot, melt butter over low heat.
2. Add carrots, celery, onions and pepper.
3. Cook and stir over medium heat about 5 minutes.
4. Add mushrooms and cook 2 to 3 minutes longer or until carrots are tender.
5. Add broth and heat until simmering.
6. Add chicken and noodles.
7. Simmer 2 to 3 minutes longer.
8. Garnish with chopped dill and serve.

Just What the Doctor Ordered

Cream of Cannabis Soup

SERVINGS	Makes 6 cups
RECOMMENDED DOSAGE	1 1/2 teaspoons of marijuana butter
PREPARATION TIME	5 minutes
COOKING TIME	45 to 50 minutes
INGREDIENTS	2 large leeks 2 tablespoons butter 4 cups ready-to-serve chicken broth 2 medium potatoes peeled and diced 1/2 teaspoon salt 1/2 teaspoon pepper 1 pound asparagus 1/2 cup whipping cream

DIRECTIONS:

1. Trim the roots and the leaves from leeks, leaving only the white and about 2 inches of the green sections.
2. Rinse well, split lengthwise and slice crosswise (about 1/2-inch thick). Sauté leeks in butter in Dutch oven over low heat for about 10 minutes or until softened.
3. Stir in chicken broth, potatoes, salt and pepper and bring to a boil over high heat.
4. Meanwhile trim off tips (about 1 1/2 inches) from asparagus: reserve for garnish.
5. Trim off and discard woody stem ends.

73

6. Chop remaining asparagus into 1-inch pieces and add to boiling soup.
7. Reduce heat and simmer uncovered about 10 minutes or until vegetables are tender.
8. Transfer soup to work bowl of food processor or blender; process until pureed.
9. Return soup to clean saucepan.
10. Stir in cream and heat throughout.
11. To prepare asparagus for garnish, bring salted water to boil in a small saucepan.
12. Add reserved asparagus tips and cook about 3 to 5 minutes or until just tender.
13. Drain well.
14. Garnish each serving with asparagus tips.

Good to the Last Drop

Asparagus Hash

SERVINGS	Makes 4 servings
RECOMMENDED DOSAGE	2 1/2 teaspoons of marijuana flour or 1 teaspoon of marijuana butter
PREPARATION TIME	30 minutes
COOKING TIME	30 minutes
INGREDIENTS	White Sauce: 4 teaspoons butter 4 tablespoons all-purpose flour 1 1/2 cups milk 1 teaspoon salt 1/2 teaspoon ground black pepper Casserole: 1/2 cup dry bread crumbs, browned in butter 30 asparagus tips 4 hard-cooked eggs, chopped

DIRECTIONS:

1. Melt butter in a small pan over medium low heat; stir in flour, then milk.
2. Cook until thickened and season with salt and pepper. This is your white sauce.
3. Spread 1/2 of the browned bread crumbs in the bottom of a 9x13 inch baking dish.

4. Add alternating layers of asparagus and chopped egg.
5. Pour white sauce over all and top with remaining breadcrumbs.
6. Bake in preheated oven for 30 minutes (350°F/175°C).

Tip Your Hat to this Mouthwatering Meal

Baked Scallops

SERVINGS	Makes 4 servings
RECOMMENDED DOSAGE	1 teaspoon of marijuana butter
PREPARATION TIME	10 minutes
COOKING TIME	20 minutes
INGREDIENTS	4 tablespoons butter, melted 1 1/2 pounds bay scallops, rinsed and drained 1/2 cup seasoned dry bread crumbs 1/2 teaspoon of chili powder 1 teaspoon onion powder 1 teaspoon garlic powder 1/2 teaspoon paprika 1 teaspoon dried parsley 2 cloves garlic, minced 1/4 cup grated Parmesan cheese

DIRECTIONS:

1. Preheat oven to 400°F/200°C.
2. Pour melted butter into a 2-quart oval casserole dish.
3. Distribute butter and scallops evenly inside the dish.
4. Combine the breadcrumbs, onion powder, garlic powder, paprika, chilies, parsley, minced garlic and Parmesan cheese.
5. Sprinkle this mixture over the scallops.
6. Bake until scallops are firm, about 20 minutes.

You'll Seafood in a Whole New Light

Chapter 7

Main Courses

Turkey Pot Pies

SERVINGS	Makes 6 servings
RECOMMENDED DOSAGE	3 teaspoons of marijuana flour or 1 1/2 teaspoons of marijuana butter
PREPARATION TIME	35 minutes
COOKING TIME	35 minutes
INGREDIENTS	2 cans (13 3/4 oz each) ready-to-serve chicken broth 1 cup water 1 fresh skinless and boneless turkey breast (about 1 1/3 pounds) 3 tablespoons butter, divided 1 package (10 oz) frozen pearl onions, thawed and drained 1/2 teaspoon sugar 1/4 cup all-purpose flour 2 1/2 cups milk 1/2 teaspoon dried marjoram, crushed 1 package (10 oz) frozen petite peas (thawed and drained) 2 cups carrots, peeled and julienne cut pie crust pastry for single-crust pie 1 egg and 1 tbsp water, beaten together

DIRECTIONS:

1. Preheat oven to 400°F/200°C.
2. Heat chicken broth and 1 cup water in Dutch oven over high heat. Bring to a boil.
3. Add turkey and water to cover; reduce heat to low

and simmer uncovered, about 25 minutes per pound (25 to 30 minutes) or until turkey is cooked through.

4. Remove turkey from broth; let stand until cool enough to handle.
5. Cut turkey into cubes and set aside.
6. Skim and discard fat from broth.
7. Strain broth and measure 1 cup for sauce (reserve remainder for another use).
8. Melt 1 tablespoon butter in large saucepan; add onions and sugar; reduce heat to medium and sauté 3 minutes.
9. Remove onions. Stir remaining 2 tablespoons butter and flour into saucepan.
10. Cook 1 to 2 minutes or until mixture is bubbly and slightly golden, stirring constantly.
11. Whisk in milk and 1 cup of reserved broth; cook until thickened, stirring constantly.
12. Season with marjoram, salt, and pepper.
13. Stir in cubed turkey, onions, peas, and carrots. Remove from heat.
14. Divide turkey mixture among six 2-cup baking dishes or ramekins.
15. Using a pastry wheel or knife, cut pie pastry into strips.
16. Brush rim of each ramekin lightly with egg mixture.
17. Arrange pastry strips decoratively on top of turkey mixture; press to adhere around edges. Bake 10 minutes.
18. Reduce oven temperature to 350°F/175°C and bake 25 minutes or until filling is bubbling and crusts are golden.

Gobble One Down Today

Sautéed Halibut with Special Seasoning

SERVINGS	Makes 4 servings
RECOMMENDED DOSAGE	3 teaspoons of marijuana flour or 1 1/2 teaspoons of marijuana butter
PREPARATION TIME	3 minutes
COOKING TIME	8 minutes
INGREDIENTS	1 1/2 pounds fresh halibut filets, about 3/4 to 1-inch thick salt and pepper flour 1/2 cup (4 ounces) clarified butter 1/4 cup fresh lemon juice 1/4 cup fresh orange juice 2 tablespoons fresh lime juice 1 tablespoon minced parsley

DIRECTIONS:

1. Lightly season halibut filets to taste with salt and pepper and lightly coat with flour.
2. In large skillet, heat butter over medium heat until hot, watching carefully so it does not burn.
3. Add fish to skillet and cook over high heat until tender, about 4 to 5 minutes on each side.
4. Place fish on a platter and keep warm in oven.
5. Add juices and parsley to butter in skillet. Cook over medium heat, 2 to 3 minutes.
6. Drizzle over halibut and serve with steamed green beans.

The Marijuana Makes it Special...

Chicken and Asparagus Fettuccini Surprise

SERVINGS	Makes 4 servings
RECOMMENDED DOSAGE	3 teaspoons of marijuana flour or 1 1/2 teaspoons of marijuana butter
PREPARATION TIME	10 minutes
COOKING TIME	15 minutes
INGREDIENTS	12 oz dry fettuccine pasta 2 cups fresh asparagus, trimmed and cut into 2 1/2 inch pieces 1/2 cup butter 2 cups half-and-half cream 3/4 cup grated Parmesan cheese 1/4 teaspoon garlic powder 1/4 teaspoon ground black pepper 1 pinch cayenne pepper 1/2 pound skinless, boneless chicken breast halves - cooked and cubed

DIRECTIONS:

1. Cook the fettuccini according to package directions, adding the asparagus during the last 5 minutes of cooking.
2. While the pasta is cooking, heat the butter and cream in a large saucepan over medium heat until butter is melted and mixture starts to bubble.
3. Stir in the cheese, garlic powder, ground black

pepper, and cayenne pepper. Continue cooking over
medium heat until mixture is thickened and bubbly.
4. Stir in the chicken.
5. Drain the pasta and asparagus; combine with the sauce
and toss to coat evenly. Serve immediately with additional Parmesan cheese, if desired.

Surprise!

He-Man Quiche

SERVINGS	Makes 6-8 servings
RECOMMENDED DOSAGE	4 teaspoons of marijuana flour or 2 1/2 teaspoons of marijuana butter
PREPARATION TIME	15 minutes
COOKING TIME	50-55 minutes
INGREDIENTS	3 tablespoons butter, room temperature 2 medium onions, finely chopped 1/4 pound fresh mushrooms, sliced 1/2 pound hot Italian sausage, casings removed 1 refrigerated folded piecrust (from a 15 oz package) 2 cups (8 oz) shredded Colby-Jack cheese blend, divided 1 1/2 cups heavy cream 3 eggs

DIRECTIONS:

1. Melt butter in a large skillet over medium heat. Add onions and mushrooms, sauté until tender (about 10 minutes); remove from heat. Place in a bowl and set aside.
2. Add sausage to skillet. Stirring occasionally, sauté until crumbled and cooked through. Drain and stir onion/mushroom mixture into pan with sausage.

3. Unfold piecrust and place in greased, 8 inch round cake pan, pressing firmly against pan to form crust; flute, if desired. Sprinkle half the cheese over the crust.
4. Top with sausage mixture, then sprinkle with remaining cheese.
5. In a medium bowl, whisk together cream and eggs.
6. Pour over cheese and sausage, then bake for 50 to 55 minutes, or until a knife inserted in the center comes out clean.
7. Cool for 10 minutes before slicing and serving.

This Dish is Pot-ent

Snappin' Lobster Casserole

SERVINGS	Makes 4 servings
RECOMMENDED DOSAGE	3 teaspoons of marijuana flour or 1 1/2 teaspoons of marijuana butter
PREPARATION TIME	20 minutes
COOKING TIME	25 minutes
INGREDIENTS	3 tablespoons butter 1 pound raw lobster meat, cut into bite-size pieces 3 tablespoons all-purpose flour 3/4 teaspoon dry mustard salt to taste ground black pepper to taste 1 cup heavy cream 1/2 cup milk 3 slices bread, crust removed

DIRECTIONS:

1. Preheat oven to 350°F/175°C.
2. Lightly grease a 2-quart baking dish.
3. In a medium sized pot, melt the butter and slowly sauté the lobster meat until it starts to change color. Do not cook too long or too fast, or the lobster meat will toughen.
4. With a slotted spoon, remove lobster meat from pan and set aside.

5. To the remaining butter in the pot, stir in the flour, dry mustard.
6. Add salt and pepper to taste. Pour in cream and milk slowly, stirring constantly; cook until thickened.
7. Return lobster meat to the cream mixture. Tear the trimmed slices of bread into small pieces and add to the mixture and stir.
8. Pour the mixture into prepared baking dish, and bake in preheated oven for 20 to 25 minutes or until bubbly and delicately browned.

Dig Your Claws into this Fabulous,
Five-Star Meal

Chapter 8

Vegetarian

Mushrooms Stuffed with Silly Spinach

SERVINGS	Makes 12 mushrooms, 6 servings
RECOMMENDED DOSAGE	1-1/2 teaspoons of marijuana butter
PREPARATION TIME	15 minutes
COOKING TIME	45 to 50 minutes
INGREDIENTS	2 tablespoons butter 1 (10 oz) package frozen chopped spinach 12 large mushrooms 3 tablespoons butter 2 tablespoons finely chopped onion 2 cloves garlic, peeled and minced 3/8 cup heavy cream 1/4 cup grated Parmesan cheese salt and pepper to taste 2 tablespoons butter, melted

DIRECTIONS:

1. Preheat oven to 400°F/200°C.
2. Butter a 9 x 13-inch baking dish with 2 tablespoons butter.
3. Place frozen spinach in a medium saucepan with 1/4 cup water.
4. Bring water to a boil, then reduce heat to medium and cook spinach covered for 8 to 10 minutes.

5. Uncover and stir.
6. Remove from heat and drain.
7. Remove stems from mushrooms and arrange caps in the baking dish. Finely chop stems.
8. Melt 3 tablespoons butter in a medium saucepan over medium heat, and mix in onion and garlic.
9. Cook 5 minutes, or until tender, then mix in spinach, chopped mushroom stems and heavy cream.
10. Bring cream to a boil.
11. Remove from heat and mix in Parmesan cheese, salt and pepper.
12. Stuff mushroom caps generously with the mixture.
13. Drizzle with 2 tablespoons melted butter.
14. Bake 30 minutes until lightly browned.

*A Hearty Meal that will Leaf You
Wanting More...*

Mashed Pot-atoes

SERVINGS	Makes 6 servings
RECOMMENDED DOSAGE	1 1/2 teaspoons of marijuana butter
PREPARATION TIME	10 minutes
COOKING TIME	15 to 20 minutes
INGREDIENTS	5 red potatoes 5 Yukon Gold potatoes 2 tablespoons butter salt and pepper to taste 1/2 cup mayonnaise 1/2 cup prepared mustard 1/2 cup sour cream 1 stalk celery, finely chopped 1 red onion, finely diced 1 green bell pepper, chopped

DIRECTIONS:

1. Cube potatoes, peeled if desired.
2. Place potatoes in a large saucepan and cover with water.
3. Cook over medium heat until potatoes are tender.
4. Drain and place cooked potatoes in a large bowl.
5. Mash potatoes with butter and salt and pepper to taste.
6. Once mashed, stir in the mayonnaise, mustard and sour cream, mixing well.
7. Stir in the celery, onion, and green pepper.
8. Serve warm or at room temperature.

A Classic Yukon Eat Anytime

Couscous Your Consciousness

SERVINGS	Makes 6 servings
RECOMMENDED DOSAGE	1 1/2 teaspoons of marijuana butter
PREPARATION TIME	10 minutes
COOKING TIME	10 to 15 minutes
INGREDIENTS	1/2 cup couscous 1 tablespoon butter 1 red onion, chopped 1 red bell pepper, chopped 1/3 cup chopped parsley 1/3 cup raisins 1/3 cup toasted and sliced almonds 1/2 cup garbanzo beans, drained 1/2 cup creamy salad dressing 1/4 cup plain yogurt 1 teaspoon ground cumin salt and pepper to taste

DIRECTIONS:

1. Over medium-low heat, melt 1 tablespoon of butter in a saucepan.
2. Add 1/2 cup couscous and stir until evenly coated in butter.
3. Add 1 cup water, bring to boil, then reduce heat to a simmer.

95

4. Cover and cook until all the water is absorbed.
5. Set aside to cool.
6. In a salad bowl, combine the couscous, red onion, bell pepper, parsley, chick peas, and raisins and almonds if desired.
7. Stir and mix well.
8. Whisk together the salad dressing, yogurt, cumin, salt and pepper.
9. Pour the dressing over the salad; stir until well-blended, seasoning with salt and pepper. Chill and serve.

Caution: May Induce Heightened Awareness.

Eggztraordinary Casserole

SERVINGS	Makes 4 servings
RECOMMENDED DOSAGE	1 teaspoon of marijuana butter
PREPARATION TIME	10 minutes
COOKING TIME	50 minutes
INGREDIENTS	9 eggs 1 cup frozen green peas, thawed 3/4 cup diced celery 2 tablespoons chopped pimento 2 tablespoons chopped onion 1 1/2 cups dry bread crumbs 4 tablespoons butter 3/4 cup mayonnaise 1/3 cup milk 1/2 teaspoon garlic salt salt and pepper to taste 2 tablespoons butter

DIRECTIONS:
1. Preheat oven to 400°F/200°C.
2. Place eggs in a saucepan and cover with cold water.
3. Bring water to a boil; cover and remove from heat. Let eggs stand in hot water for 10 to 12 minutes.
4. Remove from hot water. Cool, peel and chop eggs
5. In a large bowl, combine the eggs, peas, celery, pimento, onion, 1 cup bread crumbs, butter, mayon-

naise, milk, garlic salt, salt and pepper.

6. Mix well and pour into a 1 quart casserole dish.
7. Melt butter and fry remaining 1/2 cup bread crumbs until lightly browned.
8. Sprinkle over casserole and bake for 30 minutes.

An Egg-cellent Addition to Any Meal

Carrot Casserole

SERVINGS	Makes 6 to 8 servings
RECOMMENDED DOSAGE	1 1/2 teaspoon of marijuana butter
PREPARATION TIME	10 minutes
COOKING TIME	45 minutes
INGREDIENTS	2 cups mashed cooked carrots 1 tablespoon butter 1 cup white sugar 1/3 cup milk 1/2 teaspoon salt 1 teaspoon ground cinnamon 1 teaspoon ground nutmeg 3 eggs 1 teaspoon vanilla extract

DIRECTIONS:

1. Preheat oven to 325°F/165°C.
2. Grease a 1-quart casserole dish.
3. Place carrots and enough water to just cover them in a small saucepan.
4. Bring the water to a boil and cook until carrots are very tender; drain well.
5. Using an electric blender or food processor, mash carrots to a smooth consistency.
6. In a large mixing bowl, combine carrots and butter;

stir well.

7. Mix in sugar, milk, salt, cinnamon, nutmeg, eggs, and vanilla.

8. Pour mixture into prepared casserole dish.

9. Bake the casserole 20 to 30 minutes, or until set.

Always a Grate Choice

Broccoli and Sun-Dried Tomato au Ganja

SERVINGS	Makes 4 to 6 servings
RECOMMENDED DOSAGE	3 teaspoons of marijuana flour or 1-1/2 teaspoons of marijuana butter
PREPARATION TIME	15 minutes
COOKING TIME	45 minutes
INGREDIENTS	3/4 lb broccoli florets 2 tablespoons unsalted butter 2 1/2 tablespoons all purpose flour 1 2/3 cups skim milk, warm 1/3 cup grated Parmesan cheese 1/3 cup Swiss cheese, grated 1/2 teaspoon salt optional 1/4 lb firm light tofu, patted dry and finely chopped 1/4 cup sun dried tomatoes, soaked if not oil-packed 2/3 cup dry seasoned breadcrumbs

DIRECTIONS:

1. Preheat oven to 375°F/190°C.
2. Place broccoli in a steamer basket over boiling water.
3. Cover saucepan and steam 6 to 8 minutes or until broccoli is bright green and almost tender.
4. Rinse under cold water and drain thoroughly.

101

5. Chop coarsely and set aside.
6. Melt butter in a heavy saucepan over low heat.
7. Stir in flour and cook 3 minutes, stirring constantly, until mixture starts to bubble.
8. Gradually whisk in warm milk.
9. Bring to a boil over medium high heat, whisking constantly.
10. Reduce heat to medium and simmer 4 minutes or until mixture begins to thicken.
11. Stir in Parmesan and Swiss cheese until cheese melts.
12. Season with salt and pepper to taste.
13. Remove from heat and set aside.
14. Combine chopped broccoli with tofu and sun dried tomatoes in a buttered shallow baking dish.
15. Pour cheese sauce over broccoli and tofu mixture.
16. Sprinkle with breadcrumbs.
17. Bake 25 minutes or until crumbs are golden and mixture is bubbly.

G.W.'s Favorite

Corny Casserole

SERVINGS	Makes 8 servings
RECOMMENDED DOSAGE	2 teaspoons of marijuana butter
PREPARATION TIME	5 minutes
COOKING TIME	30 minutes
INGREDIENTS	1/4 cup butter 2 (3 oz) packages cream cheese 1 (11.25 oz) can whole kernel corn, drained 1 (15 oz) can cream-style corn 1 (4 oz) can chopped green chilis 1/2 cup chopped onion 1 (6 oz) can French-fried onions

DIRECTIONS:

1. Preheat oven to 350°F/175°C.
2. In a medium size bowl, cream together butter and cream cheese.
3. Mix in whole kernel corn, cream-style corn, chilis, chopped onions, and 1/2 can of the French-fried onions.
4. Pour mixture into a 1 quart casserole dish.
5. Bake for 15 minutes.
6. Remove from oven and sprinkle the remaining French-fried onions over the top of the casserole.
7. Return to the oven and bake an additional 15 minutes.

You'll Nibblet All Night Long

Primeval Pasta

SERVINGS	Makes 4 servings
RECOMMENDED DOSAGE	1 teaspoon of marijuana butter
PREPARATION TIME	10 minutes
COOKING TIME	20 minutes
INGREDIENTS	1 (8 oz) package fresh fettuccini 4 tablespoons butter 3 cloves garlic, crushed 1 (8 oz) package sliced mushrooms 1/2 medium onion, chopped 10 oz marinated artichoke hearts 2/3 (8 oz) jar sun-dried tomatoes, packed in oil 1 (2 oz) can sliced black olives, drained 1 teaspoon black pepper 1 ripe tomato, chopped 2 tablespoon lemon juice 1 cup dry white wine 1 cup Parmesan cheese

DIRECTIONS:

1. Cook pasta in boiling water until done. Drain.
2. Melt butter over medium heat in a large saucepan.
3. Sauté onions, mushrooms, and garlic until tender.
4. Stir in sundried tomatoes, olives, artichoke hearts,

wine, and lemon juice.
5. Bring to a boil; cook until liquid is reduced by a third, about 4 minutes.
6. Toss pasta with sauce.
7. Top with tomatoes and cheese, add salt and pepper to taste, and serve.

Get Back to the Stoned Age

Veg-Out Stoner Pie

SERVINGS	Makes 4 to 6 servings
RECOMMENDED DOSAGE	3 teaspoons of marijuana flour or 1 1/2 teaspoons of marijuana butter
PREPARATION TIME	20 minutes
COOKING TIME	1 hour and 45 minutes
INGREDIENTS	5 russet potatoes, peeled and cut into thirds 2 tablespoons butter 1 1/2 teaspoon salt ground black pepper to taste 2 cups milk 3 cups water 1/2 cup kasha (toasted buckwheat groats) 2 tablespoons butter 2 cups chopped onion 2 cloves garlic, minced 2 carrots, diced 2 cups fresh sliced mushrooms 1 1/2 tablespoons all-purpose flour 1 cup whole corn kernels, blanched 3 tablespoons chopped fresh parsley

DIRECTIONS:

1. Gently boil potatoes in a large pot of water for 20 minutes, or until tender; drain, and return to the pot.

106

2. Mash potatoes with 2 tablespoons butter, 3/4 teaspoon salt, and 1/2 cup milk until fairly smooth; set aside.
3. In a saucepan, bring 1 1/2 cups water with 1/2 teaspoon salt to a boil.
4. Stir in kasha; reduce heat, and simmer, uncovered, for 15 minutes.
5. Add 1 1/2 cups more water and bring to a boil.
6. Cover and remove from heat; let stand for 10 minutes.
7. In a large saucepan, melt 2 tablespoons of butter or margarine over medium heat.
8. Add onions, garlic, and carrots; sauté until the onions soften.
9. Add mushrooms; cook and stir for 3 to 4 minutes.
10. Sprinkle flour over vegetables; stir for 2 minutes, or until flour starts to brown.
11. Pour remaining 1 1/2 cups milk over the vegetables, and increase heat to high.
12. Stir with a whisk until sauce is smooth.
13. Reduce heat, and simmer for 5 minutes.
14. Stir in corn, 1/4 teaspoon salt, and black pepper to taste.
15. Mix together vegetable mixture and kasha mixture in a large bowl.
16. Spoon into a buttered 10 inch pie pan, and smooth with a spatula.
17. Spread mashed potatoes over top, leaving an uneven surface.
18. Bake in a preheated (350°F/175° C) oven for 30 minutes.
19. Garnish with the chopped parsley and serve.

The Perfect Meal for All Couch Potatoes

Enchanted Cottage Cheese

SERVINGS	Makes 10 servings
RECOMMENDED DOSAGE	1 1/2 teaspoons of marijuana butter
PREPARATION TIME	10 minutes
COOKING TIME	30 minutes
INGREDIENTS	1 (16 oz) container cottage cheese 2 tablespoons butter 1 cup oats, or more for consistency 4 oz saltine crackers, crushed 1 (4 oz) package round crackers, crushed 4 eggs 1 tablespoon dried sage 1 tablespoon dried oregano 1 tablespoon garlic powder 1 (10.75 oz) can cream of mushroom soup 2/3 cup milk 1 cup sliced mushrooms

DIRECTIONS:

1. Preheat oven to 350°F/175°C.
2. Lightly grease a 9 x 13-inch baking dish.
3. In a large bowl, combine cottage cheese, butter, oatmeal, salted crackers, round crackers, eggs, sage, oregano, garlic powder, mushroom soup, milk, and mushrooms. Mix well and spoon into the prepared baking dish.
4. Cover and bake for 30 minutes.

Fairy Tales Do Come True!

Chapter 9

More Desserts

Going Bananas

SERVINGS	Makes 4 servings
RECOMMENDED DOSAGE	3 teaspoons of marijuana flour or 1 1/2 teaspoons of marijuana butter
PREPARATION TIME	3 minutes
COOKING TIME	5 minutes
INGREDIENTS	1 1/4 cup butter 2/3 cup dark brown sugar 3 1/2 tablespoons rum 1 1/2 teaspoons vanilla extract 1/2 teaspoon ground cinnamon 3 bananas, peeled and sliced lengthwise and crosswise 1/4 cup coarsely chopped walnuts 1 pint vanilla ice cream

DIRECTIONS:

1. In a large, deep skillet, melt butter over medium heat.
2. Stir in sugar, rum, vanilla, and cinnamon.
3. When mixture begins to bubble, place bananas and walnuts in pan.
4. Cook until bananas are hot, 1 to 2 minutes.
5. Serve at once over vanilla ice cream.

A Peel-Good Recipe

Decadent Chocolate Bud Cake

SERVINGS	Makes 4 servings
RECOMMENDED DOSAGE	3 teaspoons of marijuana flour or 1 1/2 teaspoons of marijuana butter
PREPARATION TIME	10 minutes
COOKING TIME	25-30 minutes
INGREDIENTS	2/3 cup boiling water 1/3 cup unsweetened cocoa powder 3/4 cup and 2 tablespoons and 2 teaspoons all-purpose flour 1/4 teaspoon baking soda 1/8 teaspoon baking powder 1/8 teaspoon salt 1/3 cup butter, softened 3/4 cup white sugar 1 1/3 eggs 1/2 teaspoon vanilla extract

DIRECTIONS:

1. Preheat oven to 350°F/175°C.
2. Grease three 9-inch round cake pans.
3. In medium bowl, pour boiling water over cocoa, and whisk until smooth. Let mixture cool.
4. Sift together flour, baking soda, baking powder and salt; set aside.
5. In a large bowl, cream butter and sugar together

until light and fluffy.
6. Beat in eggs one at time, then stir in vanilla.
7. Add the flour mixture alternately with the cocoa mixture. Spread batter evenly between the three prepared pans.
8. Bake for 25 to 30 minutes. Cool.

Perfect for You and Your Buds

Apples and Green Sauce

SERVINGS	Makes one 8-inch cake that serves 10
RECOMMENDED DOSAGE	5 teaspoons of marijuana flour or 3 teaspoons of marijuana butter
PREPARATION TIME	15 minutes
COOKING TIME	55 minutes
INGREDIENTS	1 cup white sugar 1/4 cup butter 2 large apples 2 eggs 1 cup all-purpose flour 1/4 teaspoon salt 1 teaspoon baking soda 1/2 teaspoon ground nutmeg 1/2 teaspoon ground cinnamon 1/2 cup butter 1 cup white sugar 1/2 cup heavy whipping cream 1 1/2 teaspoons vanilla extract

DIRECTIONS:

1. Preheat oven to 350°F/175°C.
2. Peel, core, and grate the apples.
3. Cream together 1 cup sugar and 1/4 cup butter or margarine; stir in the grated apples and eggs.
4. Sift together flour, salt, soda, nutmeg, and cinnamon; mix into the apple mixture.

5. Pour batter into an ungreased 9-inch glass pie plate.
6. Bake for 50 minutes. Remove from oven.
7. Place the remaining butter or margarine, sugar, cup cream, and vanilla in a double boiler.
8. Heat and stir until sugar has dissolved and butter or margarine has melted.
9. Serve over apple cake.

Don't Lay Off the Sauce

Budberry Jam Cake

SERVINGS	Makes 8 servings
RECOMMENDED DOSAGE	4 teaspoons of marijuana flour or 2 1/2 teaspoons of marijuana butter
PREPARATION TIME	10 minutes
COOKING TIME	25-30 minutes
INGREDIENTS	1/2 cup butter, softened 1/2 cup white sugar 3 eggs 1/2 cup buttermilk 1 1/2 cups all-purpose flour 1/2 teaspoon baking soda 1 1/2 teaspoons ground cinnamon 1 1/2 teaspoons ground allspice 1 1/2 teaspoons ground cloves 1/2 cup seedless blackberry jam

DIRECTIONS:

1. Preheat oven to 325°F/165°C.
2. Grease and flour three 9-inch pans.
3. Mix together the flour, baking soda, cinnamon, allspice and cloves; set aside.
4. In a large bowl, cream together the butter and sugar until light and fluffy.
5. Beat in the eggs one at a time. Beat in the flour mixture alternately with the buttermilk; stir in the blackberry jam.

6. Pour batter into prepared pans.
7. Bake for 25 to 30 minutes, or until a toothpick inserted into the center of the cake comes out clean.
8. Let cake cool for10 minutes, then turn out onto a wire rack and cool completely.

Jam-Packed with Flavor

Getting Fruity

SERVINGS	Makes 10 servings
RECOMMENDED DOSAGE	5 teaspoons of marijuana flour or 3 teaspoons of marijuana butter
PREPARATION TIME	10 minutes
COOKING TIME	1 hour
INGREDIENTS	1 1/3 cups and 2 tbsp packed brown sugar 2 cups and 2 tbsp all-purpose flour 2 1/4 tsp baking soda 1 tbsp, 1 1/4 teaspoons ground cinnamon 1 tbsp, 1 1/4 tsp ground cloves 1 tbsp, 1 1/4 tsp ground allspice 1 tbsp, 1 1/4 tsp ground nutmeg 2 3/4 eggs 1 tbsp, 1 1/4 tsp lemon rind 1 tbsp, 1 1/4 tsp vanilla extract 1/3 cup, 1 tsp brandy 1 cup, 1 tsp raisins 1 cup, 1 tsp chopped walnuts 1 cup, 1 tsp dried mixed fruit 1 cup, 1 tsp butter, melted 1 1/4 cups brandy

DIRECTIONS:

1. Preheat oven to 225°F/110°C.
2. Grease and flour a tube pan.
3. In a large bowl, combine sugar, flour, soda,

cinnamon, cloves, allspice and nutmeg.

4. Add eggs, lemon rind, vanilla, and 1/2 cup brandy. Mix thoroughly.

5. Stir in fruit, nuts, and melted butter; pour into prepared pan.

6. Bake for 1 hour, or until a tester inserted in the center comes out clean.

7. Cool on a wire rack.

8. Wrap cooled cake in foil.

9. Sprinkle 2 tablespoons brandy over the cake daily for 2 weeks.

Bursting With Goodness

All Choc-O-Pot Cream Pie

SERVINGS	Makes 8 servings
RECOMMENDED DOSAGE	8 grams of marijuana flour (4 tsp) or 2 1/2 teaspoons of marijuana butter
PREPARATION TIME	5 minutes
COOKING TIME	45 minutes
INGREDIENTS	1 cup all-purpose flour 1 cup white sugar 1/3 cup cocoa powder 1/2 teaspoon baking soda 1/4 cup and 2 tablespoons butter, softened 1 cup milk 1 egg CHOCOLATE FILLING 1 teaspoon vanilla extract 1 1/2 cups light cream 1/2 cup white sugar 1/4 cup cocoa powder 2 tablespoons cornstarch 1 tablespoon butter 1 teaspoon vanilla extract SATINY CHOCOLATE GLAZE 2 tablespoons water 1 tablespoon butter 1 tablespoon corn syrup 2 tablespoons cocoa powder 3/4 cup confectioners' sugar 1/2 teaspoon vanilla extract

DIRECTIONS:

1. Preheat oven to 350°F/175°C.
2. Grease and flour one 9-inch round baking pan.
3. Mix flour, sugar, cocoa and baking soda in large bowl; add butter, milk, egg and vanilla.
4. Mix on low speed until all ingredients are moistened; mix on medium speed 2 minutes.
5. Pour batter into prepared pan.
6. Bake 30 to 35 minutes or until wooden pick inserted in center comes out clean.
7. Cool 10 minutes; remove from pan to wire rack. Cool completely.
8. Prepare Chocolate Filling.
9. Cut cake into two thin layers; place one layer on serving plate and spread filling over layer. Top with remaining layer.
10. Prepare Satiny Chocolate Glaze.
11. Pour onto top of cake, allowing some to drizzle down sides.
12. Refrigerate until serving time; cover and refrigerate leftover cake.

DIRECTIONS FOR CHOCOLATE FILLING:

1. Stir together sugar, cocoa and cornstarch in medium bowl; gradually stir in light cream.
2. Cook over medium heat, stirring constantly until mixture thickens and begins to boil.
3. Boil 1 minute, stirring constantly.
4. Remove from heat and stir in butter and vanilla.
5. Press plastic wrap directly onto surface. Cool completely.

DIRECTIONS FOR SATINY CHOCOLATE GLAZE:

1. Heat water, butter and corn syrup in small pan until mixture boils.
2. Remove from heat; immediately stir in cocoa.
3. Gradually whisk in powdered sugar and vanilla until mixture is smooth. Cool slightly.

Feed Your Greed

Chapter 10

Drinks

Over the last several years, flavored alcohol has become very popular and cannabinoids dissolve well in alcohol. Generally, the stronger the alcohol content the better. Grain alcohol is pure alcohol—odorless, tasteless, and very potent. At 190 proof, grain alcohol makes an extremely strong brew that I recommend only be used in moderation. I prefer to use vodka. Most mid-level vodkas are now triple-filtered, which helps to make them purer. Fewer impurities mean less of a hangover.

BASIC MARIJUANA ALCOHOL (VODKA)

Probably one of the easiest ways to process your leaf, marijuana alcohol can be used to create an intoxicating and mouthwatering array of beverages. For best results, marijuana alcohol should be prepared two full weeks before using.

RECOMMENDED DOSAGE	1 to 2 oz. per drink
PREPARATION TIME	5 minutes
COOKING TIME	5 minutes to mix, 1 to 2 weeks to dissolve

1. Simply take one bottle of vodka and drain approximately a quarter of the liquid.
2. Trim leaves of all stems and add the leaves to the bottle.
3. Store this mixture in a cool dark place, allowing at

126

least one week for the cannabinoids to dissolve. I recommend waiting two full weeks to ensure the maximum effect. You can use your favorite liqueur instead of vodka but please remember not to drink too much! I'd recommend 1 of these cocktails and 2 at the maximum. After that, switch to something else.

VLAD THE INHALER'S VODKA
1 oz of Vodka
1/2 oz of Gin
1/2 oz of Light Rum
1/2 oz of Tequila
2 dashes of cola so you can see when you get to the bottom of the glass
Juice of 1/2 lemon
DIRECTIONS:
1. Combine the ingredients and pour over ice in a highball glass.
2. Garnish with a slice of lemon.

MARY JANE'S MARTINI
2 oz Vodka
1 1/2 oz of Apple Barrel Schnapps
3 drops of Midori
DIRECTIONS:
1. Shake with ice and strain.
2. Garnish with a slice of green apple and enjoy!

BOURBON HIGH

2 oz. Bourbon
Ginger Ale or Club Soda

DIRECTIONS:

1. Fill Highball glass with bourbon, ginger ale or club soda, and ice cubes.
2. Add ice and twist of lemon peel, if desired, and stir.

MARIJUANA TINCTURE

Tinctures are very concentrated, so a dose may be only a few drops or a teaspoon or two. For the best results it is important to use pure alcohol like Everclear, which is 95%. Vodka is good, but when it says 40%, it means that the rest is water.

DIRECTIONS:

1. Chop up your leaf. Roughly 1 inch is a good size.
2. Fill a large Mason jar with the chopped leaf.
3. Cover with pure alcohol and close lid tightly.
4. Store in a cool dark place for four weeks.
5. Shake the container for a minute or two each week to ensure optimum distribution.
6. At the end of four weeks, strain the tincture through cheesecloth or a coffee filter.

NON-ALCOHOLIC DRINKS

Milk is an excellent medium for extracting THC from your leafs and even Soya milk can be used. I personally like to flavor the milk with a little bit of honey for a sweeter taste. If you make a large amount of milk you can always freeze it for up to three months.

DIRECTIONS:

1. Add 4 cups of milk and one desert spoon of honey to a pan and heat on a low heat until almost boiling.
2. Add 2 grams of finely chopped marijuana leaf and lower heat.
3. Simmer at the low heat for at least a half hour while stirring regularly.
4. Make sure that the milk does not boil.
5. Strain the milk through cheesecloth or a coffee filter and leave to cool.

COFFEE CHAI

4 cups of milk
1 tablespoon instant or freeze-dried coffee
1/4 cup brown sugar
3 cinnamon sticks
6 cardamom pods
1/8 teaspoon grated nutmeg

1/8 teaspoon allspice
4 cinnamon sticks, optional

DIRECTIONS:
1. Combine all ingredients in a saucepan. Simmer, stirring to dissolve sugar and instant coffee, for five minutes over low heat.
2. Don't let the mixture boil.
3. Let the mixture steep off the heat for 20 to 30 minutes.
4. Pour through a clean sieve or strainer.
5. Serve either hot or cold.

CAPPUCCINO CHILL OUT
4 cups of milk
2 tablespoons instant espresso or coffee crystals
6 tablespoons sugar
Cinnamon for garnish

DIRECTIONS:
1. Stir ingredients together until coffee is dissolved.
2. Pour into a 13 x 9 inch baking pan.
3. Cover loosely with plastic wrap and freeze overnight.
4. To serve, scrape with a spoon or ice cream scoop.
5. Place in a stemmed glass and sprinkle with cinnamon.

SPACED OUT BANANA SHAKE
1 apple, peeled and cored
3 small bananas
1 large scoop of ice cream
2 cups of fresh, ice cold milk

DIRECTIONS:
1. Mix all ingredients in a blender for 30 seconds.
2. Mix the ice cream and milk, then spread chocolate topping.
3. Serve with nuts on the top.

STIR CRAZY SHAKE
3 scoops of vanilla ice cream
3 cups (750 mls) of fresh, ice cold milk
3 tablespoons of chocolate topping
DIRECTIONS:
1. Stir! Stir! Stir! Stir!

Appendix A:
Marijuana Milestones

1893 | THE INDIAN HEMP DRUGS COMMISSION concluded that total prohibition of hemp cultivation, manufacture and sale was "neither necessary nor expedient in consideration of their ascertained effects, of the prevalence of the habit of using them, of the social and religious feelings on the subject, and to the possibility of its driving the consumers to have recourse to other stimulants or narcotics which may be more deleterious..."

1912 | INTERNATIONAL OPIUM CONVENTION required that participating nations "confine to medical and legitimate purposes the manufacture, sale and use of opium, heroin, morphine and cocaine". Cannabis was not included in the Convention.

1915 | CALIFORNIA, UTAH AND TEXAS PASS LAWS TO OUTLAW POSSESSION OF MARIJUANA.

1916- | U.S. PANAMA CANAL ZONE MILITARY
1929 | INVESTIGATIONS. Based on the results of studies conducted on U.S. soldiers stationed in Central America, a panel in Panama concluded that there was no evidence that marijuana, as it was used in the Canal Zone, was a "habit-forming" drug. The panel recommended that "no steps be taken by the Canal Zone authorities to prevent its sale or use." Despite this, the U.S. Army passed an order forbidding marijuana.

1925 | THE GENEVA CONVENTION ON OPIUM AND OTHER DRUGS focused on controlling narcotics trafficking. Because of pressure from Egypt, South Africa, Turkey, and the United States, cannabis was included in the list of narcotics. Participating nations were required to "enact effective laws to limit exclusively to medical and scientific purposes the manufacture, import, sale, distribution, export and use of cannabis in the form used for medical purposes at the time."

1931 | BY 1931 A TOTAL OF 29 STATES PROHIBITED THE USE OF CANNABIS FOR NON-MEDICINAL PURPOSES. In many states a prescription was required to purchase medications containing cannabis.

1937 | THE MARIHUANA TAX ACT required that a tax of $1 per ounce be paid by all users. Penalties included a $200 fine, a 5 year prison sentence, or both. Some manufactured products, such as birdseed and rope, were exempt.

1939- | LAGUARDIA COMMITTEE REPORT. Considered by
1944 | many to be the best study of the social, legal and medical effects of marijuana, the committee concluded that marijuana was not addictive, did not cause mental or physical harm, and was not a "stepping-stone drug" or "gateway" drug.

1946 | UNITED NATIONS COMMISSION ON NARCOTICS declares that marijuana is not a threat

1951 | The United States first institutes mandatory minimums for drug convictions under THE BOGGS ACT.

133

1954	THE WORLD HEALTH ORGANIZATION declares that cannabis is medically obsolete and addictive and the United Nations Economic and Social Council issues a statement rejecting all justifications for the medicinal use of cannabis preparations.
1961	THE JOINT COMMITTEE OF THE AMERICAN BAR ASSOCIATION AND THE AMERICAN MEDICAL ASSOCIATION ON NARCOTIC DRUGS. The committee recommends relaxing controls so that physicians can prescribe and clinics can dispense narcotics. UNITED NATIONS SINGLE CONVENTION ON DRUGS. The purpose of the convention was to coordinate international narcotic control efforts. The control of cannabis was left up to individual nations.
1967	A FULL-PAGE AD SIGNED BY THE BEATLES APPEARS IN THE LONDON TIMES, declaring that "the law against marijuana is immoral in principle and unworkable in practise".
1968- 1970	THE WOOTTON COMMITTEE REPORT (UK). No evidence was found that "serious physical dangers are directly associated with the smoking of cannabis" or that smoking cannabis caused "conditions of dependence or psychosis, requiring medical treatment. The committee concluded that the "present penalties for possession and supply are altogether too high."
1970	THE U.S. COMPREHENSIVE DRUG ABUSE PREVENTION AND CONTROL ACT classified controlled substances according to their abuse potential, known effect, harmfulness and level of accepted medical use. Marijuana is classified as a "Schedule I" drug along with heroin.

1971 | THE UNITED NATIONS CONVENTION ON PSYCHO-
TROPIC SUBSTANCES established non-penal measures
for the prevention of abuse of controlled substances.

1972 | THE REPORT OF THE NATIONAL COMMISSION ON
MARIHUANA AND DRUG ABUSE (US) found that "there
is no evidence that experimental or intermittent use of
marihuana causes physical or psychological harm." The
commission recommended that personal possession be
decriminalized.
THE BAAN COMMISSION (NETHERLANDS) presented its
final report suggesting that cannabis trade below a
quarter of kilogram be judged a misdemeanor.

1973 | DRUG USE IN AMERICA: PROBLEM IN PERSPECTIVE,
NATIONAL COMMISSION ON MARIHUANA AND DRUG
ABUSE challenges the notion that marijuana causes
physical and/or psychological harm and recommends
decriminalization of marijuana possession.

1974 | A UNITED STATES SENATE REPORT ON MARIHUANA-
HASHISH EPIDEMIC and its Impact on US Security
claims that cannabis use causes brain damage,
amotivational syndrome as well as genetic and
reproductive defects.

1975 | The United States conducts two studies of the health
effects of marijuana use—one in Jamaica and the other
in Costa Rica. Neither study finds evidence of harmful
health effects.

1976 | HOLLAND ADOPTS THE NEW OPIUM LAW. This law de
facto "decriminalizes"possession of small amounts of
cannabis.

1982	AN ANALYSIS OF MARIHUANA POLICY, NATIONAL RESEARCH COUNCIL OF THE NATIONAL ACADEMY OF SCIENCE. The Committee on Substance Abuse and Habitual Behavior, composed of 18 experts in fields as diverse as medicine, psychology, public policy and law, reviewed the available data on the costs, risks, and benefits of the major policy alternatives for the control of marijuana use and supply. Based on this review, the Committee issued a statement concurring "with the judgment of the National Commission on Marijuana and Drug Abuse, rendered in 1971, that a policy of prohibition of supply only is preferable to a policy of complete prohibition of supply and use."
1988	UNITED STATES DEA DOCKET NO. 86-22, DEA Chief Administrative Law Judge, Franics L. Young, rules that cannabis "may lawfully be transferred from Schedule I to Schedule II." His judgment, based on two years of testimony and evidence submitted by the National Organization for the Reform of Marijuana Laws (NORML), the Alliance for Cannabis Therapeutics (ACT) the DEA, the National Federation for Drug-Free Youth, etc. is flatly rejected by the DEA.
1988	UNITED NATIONS CONVENTION AGAINST ILLICIT TRAFFIC IN NARCOTIC DRUGS AND PSYCHOTROPIC SUBSTANCES. Convention seeks to address the illicit traffic in narcotic drugs and psychotropic substances at an international level. To this end, it obliges signatories to prohibit the cultivation of the opium poppy, coca bush and the cannabis plant for the purpose of the production of narcotic drugs and to make criminal possession, cultivation, and purchase of narcotics for personal consumption.

| 1998 | REGULATING CANNABIS: OPTIONS FOR CONTROL IN THE 21ST CENTURY. A forum to explore effective means of regulating cannabis for medicinal and other practical uses. |

Appendix B:

Scheduling Definitions

SCHEDULING DEFINITIONS ESTABLISHED BY THE CONTROLLED
SUBSTANCES ACT OF 1970

SCHEDULE I (INCLUDES HEROIN, LSD, AND MARIJUANA)

(A) The drug or other substance has a high potential for abuse.

(B) The drug or other substance has no currently accepted
medical use in treatment in the United States.

(C) There is a lack of accepted safety for the use of the drug or
other substance under medical supervision.

SCHEDULE II (INCLUDES MARINOL, METHADONE, MORPHINE, METHAMPHETAMINE, AND COCAINE)

(A) The drug or other substance has a high potential for abuse.

(B) The drug or other substance has a currently accepted medical use in treatment in the United States or a currently accepted
medical use with severe restrictions.

(C) Abuse of the drug or other substances may lead to severe
psychological or physical dependence.

SCHEDULE III (INCLUDES ANABOLIC STEROIDS)

(A) The drug or other substance has a potential of abuse less
than the drugs or other substances in Schedules I and II.

(B) The drug or other substance has a currently accepted medical use in treatment in the United States.

(C) Abuse of the drug or other substance may lead to moderate or low physical dependence or high psychological dependence.

SCHEDULE IV (INCLUDES VALIUM AND OTHER TRANQUILIZERS)

(A) The drug or other substance has a low potential for abuse relative to the drugs or other substances in Schedule III.

(B) The drug or other substance has a currently accepted medical use in treatment in the United States.

(C) Abuse of the drug or other substance may lead to limited physical dependence or psychological dependence relative to the drugs or other substances in Schedule III.

SCHEDULE V (INCLUDES CODEINE-CONTAINING ANALGESICS)

(A) The drug or other substance has a low potential for abuse relative to the drugs or other substances in Schedule IV.

(B) The drug or other substance has a currently accepted medical use in treatment in the United States.

(C) Abuse of the drug or other substance may lead to limited physical dependence or psychological dependence relative to the

139

Bibliography

BOOKS:

Abel, A. L. (1980). Marihuana, The First 12,000 Years. New York: Plenum Press.

Chapple, S. (1984). Outlaws in Babylon: Shocking True Adventures of the Marijuana Frontier. New York: Pocket Books.

Clarke, R. C. (1998). Hashish! Los Angeles: Red Eye Press.

Flowers, T. (1995). Marijuana Herbal Cookbook. Oakland: Flowers Publishing.

Gottlieb, A.(1993). The Art and Science of Cooking with Cannabis. Berkeley: Ronin Publishing, Inc.

Kemplay, R. (1997). The Joint Rolling Handbook. Oakland: Quick American Archives.

Kemplay, R. (1998). Stir Crazy: Cooking with Cannabis. Oakland: Quick American Archives.

Mendelson, J. H. (1974). The Use of Marijuana; A Psychological and Physiological Inquiry. New York: Plenum Press.

Randall, R. C. (1998). Marijuana Rx: The Patients Fight for Medicinal Pot. New York: Thunders Mouth Press.

INTERNET RESOURCES:
www.cannabis.com/usage/dtfaq.shtml
www.drugtest.freeserve.co.uk/
www.globalchange.com/drugtest.htm
www.lindesmith.org/
www.norml.org
www.thesite.org/drugs/opinions/how_drug_tests_work.html
www.usdoj.gov/dea/pubs/sayit/myths.htm

TV RESOURCES:
Chef, BBC TV
That 70's Show, Fox

ALSO AVAILABLE AT
YOUR LOCAL BOOKSTORE

GREETINGS FROM CANNABIS COUNTRY

BY ANDRE GROSSMAN

GREETINGS FROM CANNABIS COUNTRY is a must have for enthusiasts! The book contains a collection of 30 beautifully detailed photo-postcards, taken by Andre Grossman at Trichome Technologies—the world's most sophisticated and largest marijuana growing operation. Fourteen of the potent strains of marijuana are displayed in both a colorful and playful way. The safest way to send pot through the mail, GREETINGS FROM CANNABIS COUNTRY is entertaining as well as practical!
$11.95

DON'T MISTAKE THIS ONE FOR A SIMPLE CHILD'S ALPHABET BOOK! ABC BOOK: A DRUG PRIMER by Steven Cerio, is a must-have for Ravers and Stoners alike. Come along for the ride from A-Z, and read the poems that accompany Steven's colorful psychedelic kid's-book illustrations. Each letter represents a different type of drug, and its effects are stated in poem form—some written more on the darker side than others. A lighthearted and amusing piece of work, ABC BOOK: A DRUG PRIMER is pure fun!
$12.95

STEVEN CERIO'S ABC BOOK: A DRUG PRIMER